T0413509

Community Helpers

Helping at School

by Trudy Becker

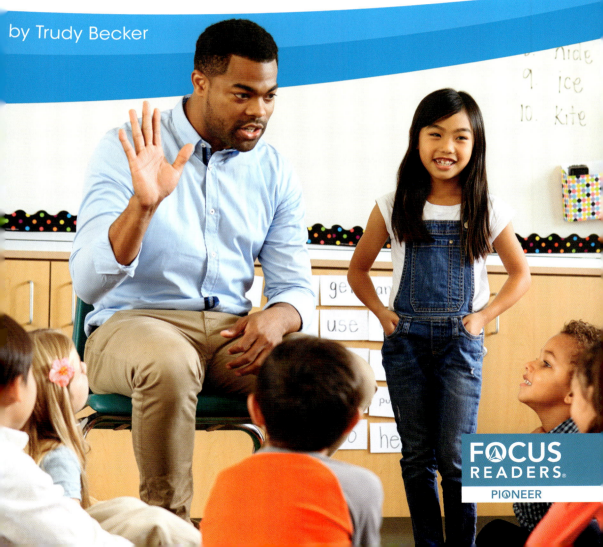

FOCUS
READERS®
PIONEER

www.focusreaders.com

Focus Readers is distributed by North Star Editions:
sales@northstareditions.com | 888-417-0195

Produced for Focus Readers by Red Line Editorial.

Photographs ©: Shutterstock Images, cover, 1, 4–5, 7, 8, 11, 17; iStockphoto, 12, 15, 18, 21

Library of Congress Cataloging-in-Publication Data
Names: Becker, Trudy, author.
Title: Helping at school / Trudy Becker.
Description: Mendota Heights, MN : Focus Readers, 2024. | Series: Community
   helpers | Includes index. | Audience: Grades 2-3
Identifiers: LCCN 2023026655 (print) | LCCN 2023026656 (ebook) | ISBN
   9798889980162 (hardcover) | ISBN 9798889980599 (paperback) | ISBN
   9798889981435 (pdf) | ISBN 9798889981022 (ebook)
Subjects: LCSH: Schools--Juvenile literature. | Helping behavior in
   children--Juvenile literature.
Classification: LCC LB1513 .B34 2024 (print) | LCC LB1513 (ebook) | DDC
   372.1042/1--dc23
LC record available at https://lccn.loc.gov/2023026655
LC ebook record available at https://lccn.loc.gov/2023026656

Printed in the United States of America
Mankato, MN
012024

About the Author

Trudy Becker lives in Minneapolis, Minnesota. She likes exploring new places and loves anything involving books.

Table of Contents

Chapter 1

Extra Help

A group of students sit at their desks. Each student has a math worksheet. They are working hard. One student has a question. He raises his hand.

An adult comes over to help. She answers the question. Then she goes to help another student. This person is not a teacher. She is a **volunteer**. She helps in the classroom.

Chapter 2

Classroom Helpers

Schools need many workers. These workers include teachers and **janitors**. But schools often have volunteers, too. Some of them help in the classroom.

Classroom helpers can do many jobs. They can **assist** students when the teacher is busy. Helpers can get things ready. They might even help teach. Having more than one adult is useful.

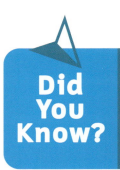

Chapter 3

All Around School

Volunteers can help in many parts of a school. Some might help in the library. They can put books on shelves. They can read to students, too.

Other volunteers help at lunch. They can arrange tables. They can hand out food. At recess, volunteers can watch over the students.

Did You Know? Some helpers work in only one part of the school. Others work in many parts.

Future and Past Teachers

Many school helpers want to be teachers someday. They practice their skills while helping. Other helpers are **retired** teachers. They still care about students. So, they help at schools in their **community**.

Outside of School

Some volunteers help outside of schools. Parking lots can be dangerous. Helpers can **direct** people. They can watch over students.

Other volunteers help on field trips. Teachers can't watch everyone at once. So, **chaperones** watch over some students. They keep students safe.

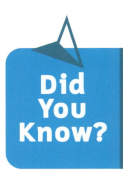

FOCUS ON
Helping at School

Write your answers on a separate piece of paper.

1. Write a sentence that explains the main idea of Chapter 4.

2. If you volunteered at a school, how would you want to help? Why?

3. Who watches students during field trips?
   A. janitor
   B. classroom helper
   C. chaperone

4. Why might teachers need classroom helpers?
   A. Students do not like teachers.
   B. There are many students and only one teacher.
   C. Teachers can't help students.

Answer key on page 24.

Glossary

assist
To help.

chaperones
People who go somewhere with a group of students to watch over them.

community
A group of people and the places where they spend time.

direct
To tell people where to go.

janitors
People whose job is to keep a building clean.

retired
No longer working.

training
Learning how to do a job.

volunteer
A person who helps without being paid.

To Learn More

BOOKS

Bassier, Emma. *Schools*. Minneapolis: Abdo Publishing, 2020.

Heos, Bridget. *Teachers in My Community*. Minneapolis: Lerner Publications, 2019.

NOTE TO EDUCATORS

Visit **www.focusreaders.com** to find lesson plans, activities, links, and other resources related to this title.

Index

Answer Key: 1. Answers will vary; **2.** Answers will vary; **3.** C; **4.** B